Viking Life
CLOTHES

Nicola Barber

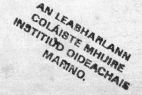

WAYLAND

Published in 2013 by Wayland

Copyright © Wayland 2013

Wayland
338 Euston Road
London NW1 3BH

Wayland Australia
Level 17/207 Kent Street
Sydney NSW 2000

Series Editor: Nicola Edwards
Series Consultant: Annette Trolle
Designer: Jane Hawkins
Picture Researcher: Kathy Lockley

British Library Cataloguing in Publication Data
Barber, Nicola.
   Viking life.
   Clothes.
   1. Vikings--Clothing--Juvenile literature.
   I. Title
   391'.0089395-dc22

ISBN: 978 0 7502 8210 9

Picture acknowledgements
© The Ashmolean Museum, University of Oxford, UK/Bridgeman Art Library,
London: 9; Geoff Dann/Dorling Kindersley/Getty Images: 8; INTERFOTO/Alamy: 17;
Werner Forman Archive: 25; Werner Forman Archive/National Museum, Copenhagen: 4, 13, 20, 28;
Werner Forman Archive/Statens Historiska Museum, Stockholm: COVER (inset), 5, 6, 16, 21, 23;
Werner Forman Archive/Universitetets Oldsaksamling, Oslo: 15, 19; Werner Forman Archive/University
Museum of National Antiquities, Uppsala: 27; Werner Forman Archive/Viking Ship Museum, Bygdoy:
11; © Annika Larsson: 12; Liz McAulay/Getty Images: COVER (main), 14 The Print Collector/Alamy:
title page, 24; Ted Spiegel/Corbis: 7, 10; © York Archaeological Trust: 18, 22, 26

The author and publisher would like to thank Torkild Waagaard for his kind permission to reproduce
his artwork of a Viking helmet on the panels in this book

Printed in China

10 9 8 7 6 5 4 3 2

Wayland is a division of Hachette Children's Books, an Hachette UK company.

www.hachette.co.uk

Contents

Words in **bold** can be found in the glossary.

The Viking world

The Vikings came from Scandinavia, the region of northern Europe that is made up of modern-day Denmark, Norway and Sweden. From the 8th to the 11th centuries, many Vikings left Scandinavia on journeys of piracy, exploration and **commerce**. This time is often called the 'Viking Age'.

At home and abroad

The word Viking comes from the **Old Norse** language, meaning 'pirate', or 'piracy'. The Vikings were superb sailors, and they used their skills to sail across seas and along rivers, **raiding** and **plundering** (or sometimes trading peaceably) as they went. However, not all Vikings were raiders or travelling traders. The people of Scandinavia were farmers and fishers, and while many Vikings set out on exciting voyages, many others remained at home.

In Scandinavia, most Vikings lived on small farms, some clustered in small villages, while others lay far from their nearest neighbours. There were busy towns too, often sited on a river or a coast so that Viking ships could dock alongside to unload their goods.

This silver pendant comes from Sweden and shows a Viking woman wearing a long dress. A shawl covers the dress, and her hair is tied back in an elegant knot.

These centres of trade included places such as Hedeby in Denmark (now in modern-day Germany), Birka in Sweden and Bergen in Norway. The Vikings also established settlements in places outside their homelands, for example Viking York – Jorvik – in northeast England.

Ibn Fadlan

Ibn Fadlan was an Arab **Muslim** from Baghdad (in present-day Iraq). In 921, Ibn Fadlan left Baghdad on a long and perilous journey to the Volga river. As he travelled, he wrote eyewitness accounts of the Vikings in Russia. These people were probably Swedish Vikings who had settled along the Russian rivers to make a living by trading goods. Ibn Fadlan describes meeting the 'Rus' – the name given to the Vikings in that area – their clothing, their customs and some of their habits that he found rather unpleasant (see page 25)!

How do we know?

We know a great deal about what the Vikings wore from evidence that has been uncovered in places such as Hedeby and Jorvik. For example, **archaeologists** have found scraps of material, elaborate jewellery, and the remains of leather shoes. After death, wealthy people were often buried in their finest clothes, so burial sites are an important source of information too.

→ Archaeologists study finds at an excavation in Hedeby.

Materials

Every set of clothes worn by a Viking man, woman or child was made by hand by the women of a family. The most common materials were wool and linen, which was made from the flax plant. Silk was also worn, but it was **imported** as luxury product for the very wealthy.

Wool

Sheep were kept on Viking farms for their wool, as well as for their milk and meat. The wool coat was cut off the sheep using large **shears**, then the wool was cleaned to remove dirt and dung. The next stage was to comb the wool to get rid of all the knots and tangles. Archaeologists have found combs with long iron teeth which were used for this purpose. To make the wool into **yarn**, a Viking woman put the mass of wool on a stick called a **distaff**. She then attached fibres from the distaff to a piece of wood or bone with a weight attached, called a **spindle**. As she spun the spindle round and down to the ground, the wool fibres were twisted into yarn.

 A modern-day model shows how Viking women spun yarn with a spindle.

Linen

Flax is a plant with a blue flower that grows naturally in southern Scandinavia. It's likely that the Vikings grew flax crops further north, in Norway and Sweden, as well as in Iceland. The fibres to make linen come from the stems of the plants. The Vikings soaked the plant stems in water, then separated out the fibres using a wooden beating tool. The fibres were combed, ready for spinning into yarn. Linen cloth was more comfortable, and less itchy against the skin than wool. It is probable that the Vikings used linen for their underclothes, and wool for heavier outer clothes. They may also have worn linen underclothes in bed.

When a Viking woman died, it was a common practice to bury her spindle whorl with her. But it is very unusual for a wooden spindle to have survived intact like this one, which comes from Hallstatt in Austria.

A Viking Object

This spindle whorl is like the ones used by Viking women. A spindle whorl had two parts, the shaft (spindle) and the weight (whorl). The whorl provided the weight to make the spindle spin round. Viking whorls were made from a variety of materials including wood, antler, bone and stone. This whorl is made from glass. The wooden shaft was where the finished yarn was wound.

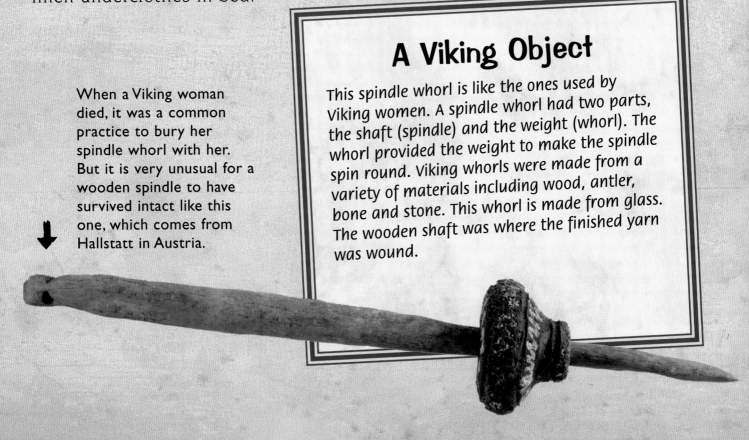

Weaving and dyeing

Once the yarn was ready, it was time to weave it into cloth. Then the cloth was either **bleached** (linen) or dyed (wool) before being cut and sewn into clothes.

A modern-day weaver in Norway adjusts the yarn on her loom. This type of upright loom is the same as the ones used by the Vikings.

A Viking loom

The yarn was woven using an upright wooden frame called a **loom**, which could be leant against a wall. The frame was made from two upright pieces of wood with a beam set into two supports at the top, and another piece of wood across the bottom. Lengths of yarn hung **vertically** from the beam to the bottom of the frame, weighted down by stones or weights made from clay to keep them taut. These were the **warp** threads. The weaver passed another thread of yarn **horizontally** between the warp threads. This horizontal thread was the **weft**. The warp and the weft threads were woven together on the loom to create different patterns in the cloth.

Dyeing the cloth

When the cloth was ready, it was taken off the loom. Linen was difficult to dye, so it was most often left its natural colour (grey or light brown), or bleached white.

Wool was dyed many different colours. The dye was made from plants such as **madder**, various **lichens**, **weld** and **woad**. Madder produced a vivid red colour, lichens were used for purples, weld for yellow and woad for blue.

The dye was boiled up over a fire in a big container, called a vat. The woollen cloth was dipped into the dye until it was the desired colour, then left to dry. Sometimes the yarn was dyed before it was woven, allowing different coloured yarns to be woven together to make brightly patterned cloth.

A Viking Object

In the early 1900s, a Viking ship was discovered in a burial mound in Oseberg, Norway. The ship dates from the 800s, and it was full of objects including remarkably well-preserved clothes and tapestries. It is thought that the ship was the burial place of a wealthy Viking woman, who was buried with her maid (there were two female skeletons in the mound). It is possible that these tapestries once hung in the woman's home.

⬆ This fragment from the Oseberg tapestries shows wagons and horses.

Women's clothes

Making a set of clothes was a long and time-consuming process for Viking women. Once the clothes were finished, they must have been looked after carefully to make them last as long as possible.

Shift and apron-dress

Viking women wore a long under-dress or shift, made either of linen or wool. Sometimes this shift had a slit at the front of the neck which was held together with a small brooch. Over this she wore a long, usually woollen, dress. This dress was rather like an apron, with straps over the shoulders. The straps were fastened together with a pair of brooches at the front (see pages 20-21 for more about brooches). Many Viking women wore lengths of beads strung between the two brooches.

These are modern copies of richly decorated Viking clothes. These would not have been used as everyday clothing. Viking women would have worn them at special ceremonial occasions.

Keeping warm

For extra warmth, a Viking woman put on a woollen shawl or cloak over her apron-dress. The shawl or cloak was also fastened with a brooch. On her feet she wore leather shoes or boots, which would be lined with fur for the cold winters. Most Viking women wore some kind of covering on their heads, ranging from simple scarves to more elaborate caps or hats.

Long clothes?

There are very few pictures of figures in Viking art, but there are some **pendants** and other pieces of jewellery that show women and their dress. (One of these pendants is shown on page 6.) From this evidence, it seems likely that Viking women wore their clothes long, possibly trailing along the ground behind them.

Written at the time

This description of a Viking woman comes from an Old Icelandic poem called the *Rigsthula* (Song of Rig):

'The woman sat and the distaff wielded,
At the weaving with arms outstretched she worked;
on her head was a band, on her breast a smock [shift];
On her shoulders a kerchief with clasps [brooches] there was.'

⬆ This pair of gold brooches comes from Denmark. The brooches date from the 900s and were used to fasten a Viking woman's dress.

Men's clothes

Viking men wore undershirts and tunics, with breeches (trousers) to cover their legs. For warmth they wore heavy cloaks made of wool or fur.

Undershirts and tunics

Men's undershirts and tunics were carefully made out of several different parts, which were cut out and then sewn together. The cloth for an undershirt was either fine wool or linen. A heavier wool cloth was used to make a tunic. There were different styles for undershirts and tunics – some were quite narrow and well-fitted, others were fuller and wider. The sleeves were long and often extended over the man's hands. Viking tunics were usually decorated around the neck and sleeves with **braid** – narrow bands of wool woven in bright colours and patterns.

➡

A model wears typical Viking clothes: breeches, tunic, and an animal fur cloak.

Breeches and cloaks

A Viking man's undershirt and tunic came down to his thighs or his knees. Beneath this he wore breeches, sometimes tight-fitting and sometimes baggy. These breeches were held up either with a drawstring around the waist, or with a belt. On his feet, the Viking man had leather shoes, lined with fur for warmth. His heavy cloak was fastened with a cloakpin. Men wore their cloaks so that the fastening was on the shoulder, leaving the right arm free to reach for a weapon if necessary.

This Viking brooch was found at Vullum in Norway.

A Viking Object

This silver ring and pin brooch was used to fasten a man's cloak. This style of brooch was copied by the Vikings from cloakpins worn by men in Scotland and Ireland. Like the jewellery worn by women, elaborate cloakpins showed the wealth and importance of the wearer. Some cloakpins were huge, with elaborate decorations.

Warriors and weapons

Almost every Viking man carried a weapon. Slaves were not allowed to have weapons, and it was considered shameful to injure a woman in a fight.

Weapons

Weapons were expensive items, and Viking men looked after them very carefully. When a warrior died, he was often buried with his weapons or they were handed down to his sons. The most common Viking weapons were swords, axes and spears. The Vikings made large, round shields out of wood, with an iron centre and a grip for the warrior's hand. Only wealthy Vikings could afford more than one weapon, but Viking warriors had several.

The Viking warriors shown in this bronze relief from Sweden are wearing helmets topped by the figures of boars. These animals were linked with Freyja, goddess of war.

Armour

The wealthiest Vikings could afford simple helmets made from iron. The helmet fitted the head snugly and had an extra piece extending down at the front to protect the nose. To make the helmet more comfortable it's likely that it was lined with leather or sheepskin. The Vikings also made tunics out of chainmail for added protection in battle. Chainmail is made of thousands of small iron rings that interlock. However, a suit of chainmail would have been so expensive that few Vikings could have afforded one.

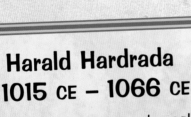

Harald Hardrada
1015 CE – 1066 CE

King Harald III of Norway, also called Harald Hardrada ('hard ruler'), was a Viking warrior. After he became king of Norway in 1047, he decided to lay claim to Denmark too. But after many years of fighting, he was forced to give up and turned his attention to England instead. He invaded England with a large force in 1066, and won his first battle against the English. But his forces were heavily outnumbered at the Battle of Stamford Bridge, and Harald himself was killed when he took an arrow through his eye. This battle is generally thought to mark the end of the Viking Age in England.

⬆ This Viking chess piece shows a warrior called a berserker biting his shield in the fury of battle. He wears a helmet and carries a sword and shield.

Shoes and accessories

We know about shoes, hats, belts and other accessories from remains that have been dug up in places such as Jorvik and Hedeby. Sometimes these remains are only fragments, but they still provide valuable evidence.

Shoes

Archaeologists at Jorvik have found several complete shoes and boots during their excavations of the Viking town. Viking shoes were often made from goatskin, although leather from calves, sheep and deer was also used. The shoes were usually ankle height, and were fastened with toggles or with leather thongs or laces.

↑ Examples of Viking shoes that have been unearthed at Jorvik.

Hats and mittens

Men's caps were made from wool, sheepskin, leather or fur. Some had a strap that went under the chin to hold them in place. Remains of hats and coats from Hedeby show that some Viking men had their hats trimmed to go with particular coats. Mittens were made from wool cloth, or by a type of single needle knitting called **nalbinding** (see page 26).

Belts

The Vikings did not have pockets in their clothes, so both men and women hung useful or valuable items from their belts. Women's belts were probably made from woven fabric. Men's belts were made from leather, with metal buckles and strap ends. Archaeologists have dug up lots of examples of beautifully decorated Viking belt buckles and strap ends, even though the leather of the belt has long since rotted away.

Men attached small **pouches** made from leather or cloth to their belts for carrying small items. Another essential object was a knife, and some men also attached a small sword as a weapon. Viking women carried keys, scissors, needles, combs and other everyday objects on their belts. These items were attached by leather thongs, or small metal chains.

A Viking Object

This elaborate piece of metalwork once covered the end of a leather belt. On the other end was a buckle. Viking men wore long belts around their middles, with the strap end hanging down. This finely decorated strap end must have belonged to a very wealthy Viking.

↑ A gold strap end, found in Norway.

Metal jewellery

For the Vikings, jewellery was an important part of everyday life. Both men and women wore a lot more jewellery than most people today.

This highly decorated silver arm ring comes from Denmark. It must have been very heavy to wear on the arm!

Status symbol

For the Vikings, fine jewellery was an indication of a person's wealth and status. Both men and women wore pins and brooches to fasten their clothes. Women also wore pendants, arm-rings (like bracelets, but worn on the arm rather than the wrist) and rings on their fingers, as well as strings of beads. The richest Vikings could afford jewellery made from gold and silver.

Cheaper metal jewellery was made from copper, bronze (a mixture of copper and tin), lead and pewter (a mixture of tin and other metals).

Brooches

The pairs of brooches worn by Viking women to fasten their apron-dresses were usually oval-shaped and decorated with elaborate patterns.

Written at the time

Ibn Fadlan (see page 7) described how the Russian Vikings turned silver Arabic coins into valuable jewellery:

'Whenever a man's wealth reaches ten thousand dirhems [Arabic coins], he has a band [neck-ring] made for his wife; if it reaches twenty thousand dirhems, he has two bands made for her... Sometimes one woman may wear many bands around her neck...'

The brooch used to fasten a woman's cloak was often in a **trefoil** (clover-leafed) shape – again highly decorated. These styles were fashionable all over the Viking world. Many Viking men fastened their heavy cloaks with beautifully decorated ring pins. This type of brooch has a ring through which the pin is hooked to prevent it from falling out.

Coins into jewellery

The Vikings imported silver coins to be turned into jewellery. The coins came from the distant lands of Arabia and the East. The Vikings had no interest in the coins for money – instead they melted the coins down and turned them into silver arm-rings, neck-rings or finger-rings.

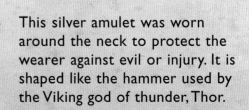

⬆ This silver amulet was worn around the neck to protect the wearer against evil or injury. It is shaped like the hammer used by the Viking god of thunder, Thor.

Beads

Viking women wore strings of beads between the two oval brooches that held up their apron-dresses. Just as her silver jewellery showed off the family's wealth, so did the number and the quality of the beads in a woman's necklace.

Amber and jet

Beads were made from a wide variety of materials including amber, jet and glass. Amber is a **fossil** – the remains of sticky **resin** from ancient pine trees. It ranges from yellow to dark orange in colour, and the Vikings prized it for its colour and smoothness. Jet is a black stone, rather like coal. It is shiny when it is polished. The only source of jet was at Whitby, on the English coast near Jorvik. The Vikings made it into jewellery in workshops in Jorvik. Both amber and jet were used to make pendants and finger-rings as well as beads.

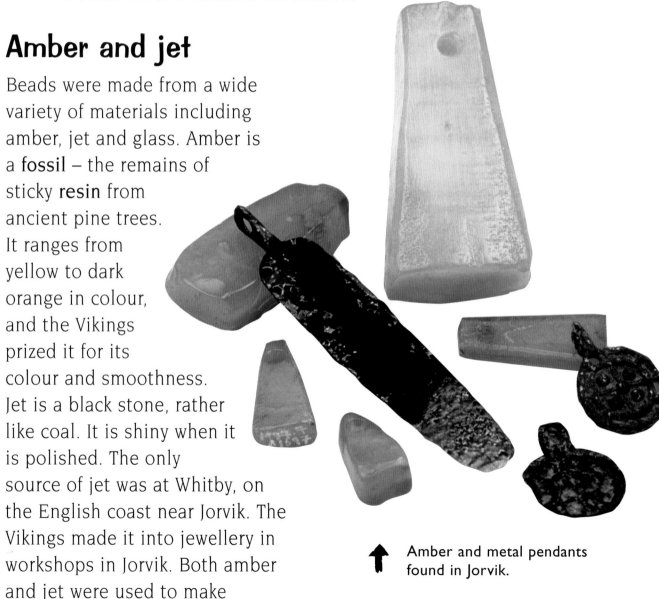

↑ Amber and metal pendants found in Jorvik.

Viking beads

Glass

Glass beads were very popular in the Viking world. They were fiddly and time-consuming to make, and therefore expensive and valuable. They came in many designs and colours. Glass-makers melted down pieces of broken glass to re-make it into beads. The Vikings imported glass to make beads, for example beautiful mosaic (multi-coloured and patterned) glass from Italy. Glass was also used to make finger-rings. Wealthy Vikings could afford beads made from imported **gemstones** such as rock crystal, a clear, colourless stone, or carnelian, which is a reddish-brown.

Hair and hygiene

Grooming and keeping clean seem to have been important in everyday Viking life. Archaeologists have found many examples of Viking combs, ear-wax scrapers, toothpicks and tweezers.

Hairstyles

We know about hairstyles from pictures and from descriptions in the **sagas** and other Viking literature. It seems that women had long hair. Girls and unmarried women often wore their hair loose or in plaits, while married women gathered their hair into a knot at the back of the head. Women wore a variety of head coverings including scarves, simple hoods with ties at the front, and thin hairbands which were tied around the head. Viking men had many different hairstyles, but it seems likely that all men grew beards and moustaches.

This Viking warrior has a neat beard and moustache.

Keeping clean

From the large numbers of combs found at Viking sites, it seems that keeping hair clean and tidy was important to the Vikings. Combs were made from animal bone or deer **antlers**. Viking women washed and cut the hair of their menfolk. The Vikings also used ear-wax scrapers to clean out their ears, and nail-cleaners to remove dirt from their nails.

The Vikings seem to have washed and bathed regularly. Many large Viking farms had separate bathhouses. In Iceland, the Vikings made use of the natural hot water that bubbled up to the surface, thanks to the **volcanic** activity beneath.

A bathing pool in Iceland, fed by water that is naturally heated by the hot rocks below.

Written at the time

Despite all the evidence to show that the Vikings took pride in their cleanliness and appearance, the Arab writer Ibn Fadlan was not impressed with the way the Russian Vikings washed:

'Every morning a girl comes and brings a tub of water, and places it before her master. In this he proceeds to wash his face and hands, and then his hair, combing it out over the vessel. Thereupon he blows his nose, and spits into the tub, and leaving no dirt behind, conveys it all into this water. When he has finished the girl carries the tub to the man next to him, who does the same...'

Luxury items

Viking trade networks extended from Scandinavia far to the east and south. The Vikings **exported** goods such as furs, amber and woollen cloth in exchange for silk, silver coins and glass.

➡

The remains of a woollen sock made by the nalbinding technique, found in Jorvik.

Socks

During the cold winters, socks helped to keep feet warm and dry. Those people who could not afford to make socks probably used moss or grass to line their shoes. Socks were made from wool using a type of knitting called nalbinding. The woollen thread was threaded and knotted to make a fabric which could be shaped into a sock, or into hats or mittens. The remains of a sock like this was found at Jorvik.

Shaggy cloaks

The Vikings made heavy men's cloaks with a type of 'fake fur' on the outside. These cloaks were made from wool, with tufts of undyed wool sewn or looped on to the outside. The tufts of wool gave the cloak a shaggy appearance, and helped to make it extra warm. These cloaks were made in Iceland, in the Western Isles (off the west coast of Scotland) and the Isle of Man.

Silk

Silk cloth came from the **Byzantine Empire**, and even from as far away as China. It was a luxury item that only wealthy Vikings could afford. Silk was most often used to make trimmings and edgings for woollen or linen clothes. At Jorvik, archaeologists have found the remains of a silk cap, made from a rectangle of silk folded and stitched up the back. It seems likely that such caps were popular with Viking women.

A Viking Object

This silk cuff was found in the grave of a Viking man in Sweden. It has been beautifully embroidered with silver thread. This style of embroidery may have been influenced by fashions from the Byzantine Empire. Another silk cuff and a silk collar were also found in the grave.

⬆ Embroidered silk from a Viking grave.

Timeline

CE

793	Vikings raid monastery of Lindisfarne, Northumbria, England
794	Viking raids on the monasteries of Jarrow and Wearmouth in England
795	Vikings raid monastery of St Columba on Iona, Scotland
800s	Vikings settle in the Orkney and Shetland Islands
c.800	Founding of Hedeby
815	Floki of Rogaland sets out from the Faroe Islands for Iceland
830s	Viking attacks on western Europe and Ireland begin
841	Vikings establish a *longphort* at Dubh-Linn (Dublin) in Ireland
843	Vikings plunder Nantes, France
844	First recorded Viking raid in Spain
850	Viking fleet lands in Kent
860	Vikings attack Constantinople
865	Arrival of a large Viking army in England
866	York is captured by a Viking army
870s	Start of mass Viking settlement of Iceland
878	King Alfred defeats the Vikings at the Battle of Edington
911	Normandy becomes a Viking territory under King Rollo
921–2	Ibn Fadlan travels from Baghdad to the Volga and describes the Swedish Vikings he meets
954	The last Viking king of Jorvik is thrown out of York
991	Vikings defeat the English army at the Battle of Maldon
c.1000	Leif Eriksson sails to North America and names it Vinland
1016	Knut becomes King of England
1042	Edward the Confessor becomes king of England
1066	Norwegian king Harald Hadrada is defeated at the Battle of Stamford Bridge. English king Harold II is defeated at the Battle of Hastings. William the Conqueror takes control of England

Glossary

antler one of the branched horns on the head of an adult deer

archaeologist a researcher who studies ancient remains

bleach to make something white

braid a thin, decorative band made out of woven threads

Byzantine Empire the Eastern Roman Empire, centred on Constantinople (modern-day Istanbul), that survived until 1453

commerce trade

distaff a stick on which wool is wound for spinning

export to send goods to another country for sale

fossil the remains of an ancient plant or animal that has been turned into stone over millions of years

gemstone a stone that is used in jewellery

horizontally describes something that moves from side to side rather than up and down

import to bring goods in from another country for sale

lichen a plant that grows on stones, walls and trees

loom a frame used for weaving

madder a plant that produces a red dye

Muslim describes a follower of Islam, the religion founded by the Prophet Muhammad

nalbinding a type of Viking knitting, done with a single needle, to create a piece of fabric

Old Norse the language spoken by Scandinavians during the Viking Age

pendant a piece of jewellery that hangs on a chain round the neck

plunder to steal goods forcibly

pouch a small purse

raid to make a surprise attack

resin a sticky substance that comes out of some plants, such as pine trees

saga a long tale of heroic achievements, usually in Old Norse or Old Icelandic

shears large scissors

spindle a long piece of wood used to wind and make yarn or thread

status describes rank or social standing

trefoil a shape with three parts, rather like a clover leaf

vertically describes something that moves or lies up and down

volcanic describes the action of volcanoes, places where hot rock from deep beneath the ground erupts through the surface

warp on a loom, the threads that hang vertically

weft on a loom, the threads that are woven horizontally

weld a plant that produces a yellow dye

woad a plant that produces a blue dye

yarn spun thread used for weaving or knitting

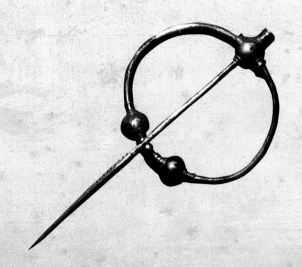

Index

Resources

History from Objects: The Vikings, Colin Malam, Wayland 2010

All about Ancient Peoples: The Vikings, Anita Ganeri, Watts, 2009

Men, Women and Children in Viking Times, Colin Hynson, Wayland, 2009

http://www.jorvik-viking-centre.co.uk/
Website of the Jorvik Viking Centre in York
http://www.bbc.co.uk/schools/primaryhistory/vikings/
BBC site for children about the Vikings
http://www.nmm.ac.uk/schools/resources/vikings-support-materials

Information and materials about the Vikings at the National Maritime Museum's website